W9-BUX-476

DISCARD

DISCARD

JUL 6 1994

JE
Ford, B.G.
Grover's Book of Cute Little
   Baby Animals

WELLSVILLE CITY LIBRARY
No._____
WELLSVILLE, KANSAS

Hello, everybodee! Would you like to come with me to the library?
GROVER

Grover's Book of Cute Little Baby Animals

by E.G. Ford

Illustrations by
Tom Leigh

Featuring Jim Henson's
Sesame Street Muppets

WELLSVILLE CITY LIBRARY
No. 3-2089
WELLSVILLE, KANSAS

A SESAME STREET/GOLDEN PRESS BOOK
Published by Western Publishing Company, Inc.
in conjunction with Children's Television Workshop.

© 1980 Children's Television Workshop.
Grover and other Muppet characters © 1980 Muppets, Inc. All rights reserved. Printed in U.S.A.
SESAME STREET®, the SESAME STREET SIGN, and THE SESAME STREET BOOK CLUB
are trademarks and service marks of Children's Television Workshop.
GOLDEN® and GOLDEN PRESS® are trademarks of Western Publishing Company, Inc.
No part of this book may be reproduced or copied in any form without written permission from the publisher.
Library of Congress Catalog Card Number: 79-91858
ISBN 0-307-23103-8

Photo Credits: From ANIMALS ANIMALS: p. 10 © Z. Leszcynski, p. 11© Michael &
Barbara Reed, p. 12 © Charles Palek 1978, p. 13 top © Gary W. Griffen, pp. 14-15 ©
Roger Minkoff, p. 16 © L.L.T. Rhodes, p. 17 © Margot Conte, p. 19 © Dagmar, p. 22 ©
M. Austerman, p. 23 © Tanaka Kojo, p. 24 © Fran Allan, p. 25 © Charles Palek, p. 26 ©
Fran Allan, Courtesy THE BETTMANN ARCHIVE: p. 13 bottom. From PHOTO
RESEARCHERS, INC.: p. 18 © Elisabeth Weiland, pp. 20-21 © Edmund Appel.

Sh-h-h

GROVER

Oh, I am so excited! I am going to borrow a book from the library.

Oh, wonderful! CUTE LITTLE BABY ANIMALS. This is the book I would like to borrow!
QUIET PLEASE

I can hardly wait to read my library book. Would you like to read it with me? You would? Oh, I am so happy!

Baby cats are called kittens.
Kittens have soft fur and sharp claws.
When kittens are happy, they purr.

Baby dogs are called puppies.
They love to run and bark and play.
Kittens and puppies make good pets.

Oh, my goodness.
They are so cute
and furry!

The baby raccoon can climb up
into its home in a hollow tree.

A baby deer is called a fawn.
A fawn's spotted coat helps it hide
in the grass.

A baby rabbit is a bunny. It has long
ears and a short fluffy tail.

Some baby animals live on the farm.
Baby sheep are called lambs.
They have soft woolly coats.

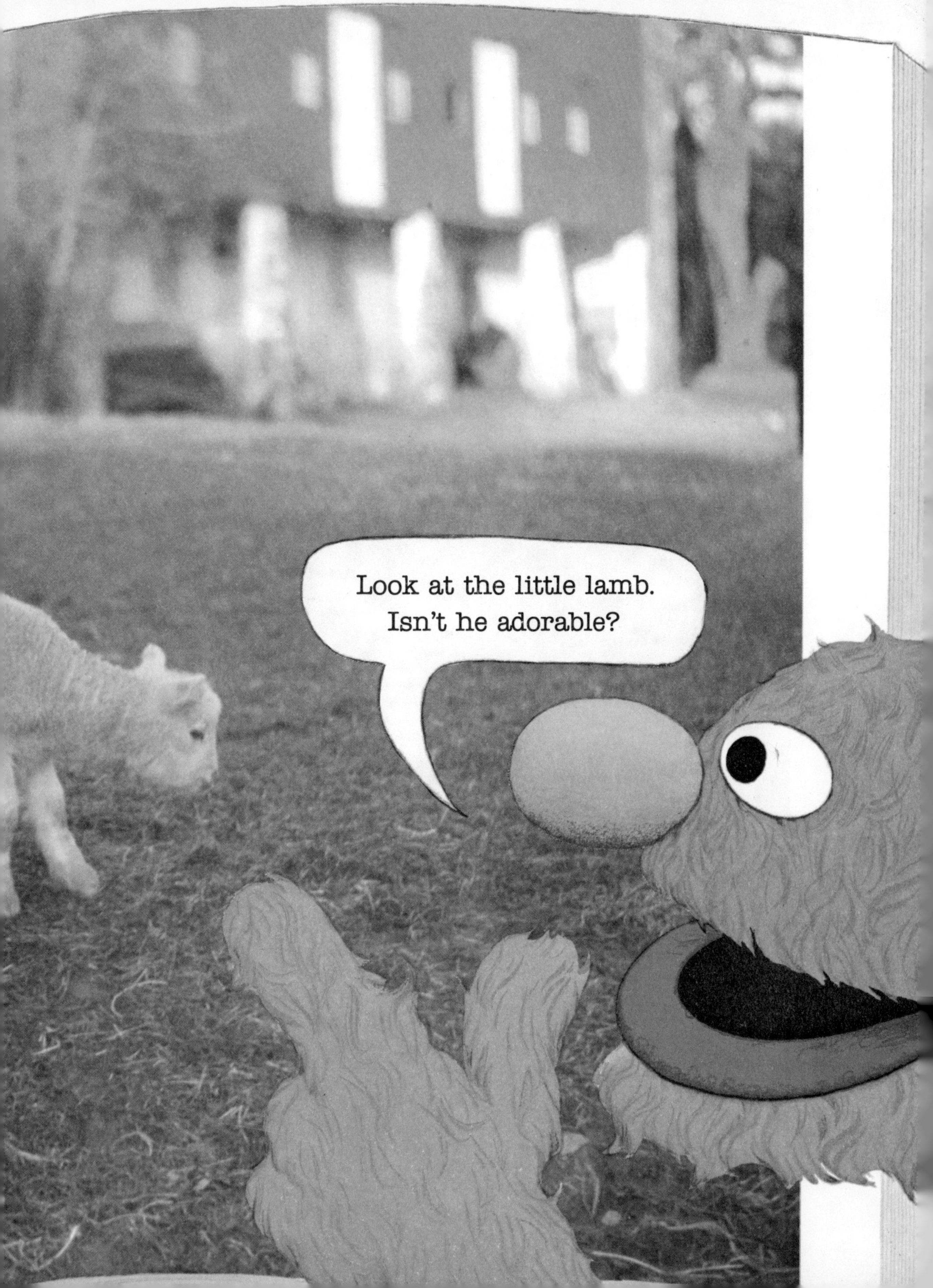
Look at the little lamb. Isn't he adorable?

Many farmers raise ducks and chickens.
Ducklings are baby ducks.
They can swim and find food a few
hours after they are born.

Chicks are baby chickens.
They are covered with fluffy yellow
feathers called down.

A newborn horse is called a foal.
Foals can run on their long, thin legs
soon after they are born.

A baby cow is called a calf.
Calves often sleep in a barn on a bed
of warm, dry hay.

Baby goats
are called kids.
Goats are good
climbers.

Oh! This mother
goat has two kids!
They are twins.

A baby kangaroo is called a joey.
It stays in its mother's pouch until
it is big enough to get around by itself.
Joeys have large feet, a strong tail,
and are very good jumpers.

The baby koala is called a cub.
Koalas spend most of their time in trees.
The mother carries her cub until it is
almost fully grown.

Baby lions are called cubs.
Lion cubs like to play.
They have very sharp
teeth and claws.

Baby bears are called cubs, too.
Bear cubs have thick fur.
Their strong claws help them
to climb trees.

A baby elephant is called a calf.
The mother elephant can use her trunk
to guide her little calf along.
Elephants can also use their trunks
to drink water or pick up food.

Look at this baby monster.
He is soft and blue and furry.
Isn't he cute and adorable?
I love <u>all</u> the little babies.
Do you want to read my book again?
Oh, joy! Let's start at the beginning!

CUTE LITTLE BABY ANIMALS

WELLSVILLE CITY LIBRARY
No._____
WELLSVILLE, KANSAS